The gentle, dry hills.   The crunchy green grass.   And the shepherds who take care of us!   Baa-aa!

For David Ford, who had faith in me

Dear Children,

The story of David and Goliath is from the Bible: 1 Samuel 17. David is a hero for several reasons: He is both willing and prepared to do what he needs to do, and he trusts God to help him.

David was the author of many psalms. A psalm can be read as a poem or sung as a song. For the songs in this book, I have taken lines from David's Psalm 23. These lines are printed in blue ink. You can read them as poetry, sing them to tunes you create, or do what I like to do, which is to sing them loosely to the tune of "Twinkle, Twinkle, Little Star."

Because David was a shepherd, I have chosen lambs to comment on the story at the bottom of the page. Please read their words last, just before you turn the page—and, if you like, help them *baa!*

Best wishes,
Jean Marzollo

I would like to thank Carol Devine Carson; Mim Galligan; Susan Jeffers; Sheila Rauch; Patricia Adams; Irene O'Garden; Judith Kurz Foster; Jennifer Contennec; Chalupa; Bunny Hoffinger; my husband, Claudio; my editors Simone Kaplan and Jennifer Hunt; art director Alyssa Morris; my agent Molly Friedrich; Rev. T. Richard Snyder; and all the children at St. Luke's R.C. School, the First Presbyterian Church of Philipstown, the Abraham Joshua Heschel School, the Westchester Jewish Center Nursery School, the Quaker Meeting in Philipstown, the Ringwood Christian School, and Nice Care Day Care.

Little, Brown and Company • Time Warner Book Group • 1271 Avenue of the Americas, New York, NY 10020
Visit our Web site at www.lb-kids.com

First Edition

Scriptures taken from the New American Standard Bible, copyright © 1995 by the Lockman Foundation

ISBN 0-316-74138-8

10 9 8 7 6 5 4 3 2 1

TWP

Printed in Singapore

The illustrations for this book were painted in watercolor and Chinese ink, then scanned and finished in Adobe Photoshop on a Power Mac G4. The text was set in Hadriano Light and Kid Print, and the display type was set in Sand.

A BIBLE STORY
Retold and illustrated by JEAN MARZOLLO

David and Goliath

BAA!

BAA!

BAA!

LITTLE, BROWN AND COMPANY

New York ~ Boston

What's the giant's name again?   Goliath!   Is he on the next page?   No. David's on the next page.   Baa!

Introduction

Long, long ago an Israelite boy named David lived with his father Jesse, his great-grandmother Ruth, and seven older brothers in Bethlehem, a small town in a hilly land called Judah. The Israelites (also called Hebrews) were a tribe of poor shepherds and farmers.

David was a shepherd. He liked that job because while he watched his sheep, he could sing and play his harp. David made up his own songs.

All of his songs were about God. David's music was so good that sometimes he was asked to sing for Saul, King of the Israelites.

The Lord is my shepherd, I shall not want. He makes me lie down in green pastures.

What does 'I shall not want' mean?   God is David's shepherd.   God takes care of him.   That's all David wants!   Baa!

David had another exceptional skill. He was outstanding at hitting targets with a sling that hurled stones. Being a shepherd gave David lots of time to practice, which was good because every so often he had to kill a lion that wanted one of David's lambs for lunch.

The Story: David and Goliath

One day, David and his family waved good-bye to David's three oldest brothers. They were leaving to help King Saul protect the land of Judah from the invading Philistine army. The Philistines were rich city people who lived along the coast. They had come to conquer the Israelites and take over their land. The Israelites didn't want that. They loved their land, their sheep, and their freedom, so they had to fight the Philistines. Every family sent men to help.

God be with you!

And all the Israelites!

'm glad David is staying home.   He needs to watch his sheep!   Find them grass and water!   Protect them from lions!   Baa!

Days passed. As David watched his sheep, he worried about the war. Had the armies started fighting yet? His family had no way of knowing. One night at supper, his father honored him with a special request.

Tomorrow, David, I would like you to take food to the Israelites' camp. Please see how your brothers are, and bring us back news!

Yes, Father!

That night, David was so nervous, he had to sing himself to sleep.

The Lord is my shepherd, I shall not want.
He makes me lie down in green pastures.

He leads me beside quiet waters.
He restores my soul . . . zzz-zz-z.

David can't sleep? He can when he pretends that he's a sleepy lamb in a pasture with God watching over him. Baa!

Early the next morning, David set out for the battleground. When he arrived, he saw Israelite soldiers marching down one hill and Philistine soldiers marching down another. David's heart began to thump. They were about to attack each other! Then, suddenly, everyone stopped. An enormous giant stepped forward from the Philistine line of soldiers. He began to shout at the Israelites!

The Israelites ran back up their hill. Quickly, David caught up with them. As he ran, he asked about Goliath and learned that Goliath had been shouting his challenge for forty days straight!

David's brothers were quite angry at him.

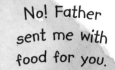

Did you run away from home?

No! Father sent me with food for you.

Who's taking care of your sheep?

Another shepherd!

Why are you asking so many questions about Goliath?

I'm trying to find out why, for forty days, NO ONE has dared to fight him!

Why are David's brothers so angry?   Maybe they're embarrassed.   David saw them run away from Goliath!   Baa!

David's questions reached the ears of King Saul, who was in his tent at the battlefield. The king asked to see David. As David entered the royal tent, he prayed to God for courage.

I may be a shepherd,
but I have *killed lions!*
I take care of my sheep,
and the Lord takes care of me.

Then may the Lord be with you, David!
Come, I'll give you my armor to wear.

King Saul gave David
his helmet, armor,
sword, and
spear. But
they didn't
fit David.

I can't use
these things.
They're too big
and too heavy!

David took off the king's armor and started down the hill toward Goliath. Between him and the giant was a small stream. Quietly, David spoke to God.

Even though I walk through the valley of the shadow of death, I will fear no evil, for You are with me.

Did Goliath hear David?   No.   Did God hear David?   Yes!   Baa!

Goliath watched suspiciously as David came toward him. He saw the boy stop at the stream and pick up five smooth stones and put them in his shepherd's bag. Goliath was insulted!

What am I, a dog that you come to fight me with five little stones? I'll feed you to the birds!

Is David afraid now?   I would be, but then I'm only a little lamb.   David's a brave shepherd!   Baa!

David crossed the stream and kept walking toward the giant.
As he walked, he took his sling out of his bag and put a
stone in it. It was just a stone, but it was good enough for
David because he knew he had another weapon, too . . .
an invisible weapon.

You come at me with
sword and spear.
But I come at you
with GOD!

Is Goliath afraid?　　　No, but he should be!　　　Baa!

David ran straight for the giant.
He twirled the sling around fast
and then let go of one end.
The stone flew out,
directly at Goliath.

BOING!

The stone hit the giant right in the
forehead and knocked
him down.

THUD!

Goliath, the mighty warrior, was dead.

Young David had won the battle for King Saul and the Israelites!
His brothers were very proud of him.

David won many battles for the Israelites, and in time, he became king himself. He was king for forty years. During his rule, Judah became part of a big, powerful kingdom called Israel. But no matter how busy King David was, he always found time to sing and write songs about God.

Surely goodness and loving kindness will follow me all the days of my life, and I will dwell in the house of the Lord forever.

That's pretty good for a shepherd to become king!   I agree!   He deserved it!   Baa-aa!   Baa!

I have a question. After David killed Goliath, did the Philistines become the Israelites' servants?   No, the Philistines ran awa